Wings of Faith

Patience and Gratitude

WINGS OF FAITH: PATIENCE AND GRATITUDE
TRANSCRIBED AND ADAPTED FROM
"WINGS OF FAITH: PATIENCE AND GRATITUDE"
BY
DR. OMAR SULEIMAN

Published by:

TERTIB PUBLISHING

Unit No. E-10-5, Jalan SS 15/4G, Subang Square,
47500 Subang Jaya, Selangor, Malaysia
+603-5612-2407 (office) / +6017-399-7411 (mobile)
info@tertib.press
www.tertib.press
@tertibpress (Facebook & Instagram)

Author	:	Dr. Omar Suleiman & Muḥammad al-Shareef
Transcriber & Editor	:	Norashikin Azizan
Proofreader	:	Arisha Mohd Affendy Nadiah Mohamed Aslam Ahmed Elbenni
Cover designer	:	Abdul Adzim Md Daim
Typesetter	:	Abdul Adzim Md Daim

WINGS OF FAITH

First Edition: July 2022
Second Edition: August 2022
Third Edition: July 2023
Fourth Edition: July 2024

Perpustakaan Negara Malaysia Cataloguing-in-Publication Data
Omar Suleiman
Wings of Faith : Patience and Gratitude / OMAR SULEIMAN, MUHAMMAD AL-SHAREEF.
ISBN 978-967-2844-19-8
1. Faith (Islam).
2. Patience--Religious aspects--Islam.
3. Gratitude--Religious aspects--Islam.
4. Religious life--Islam.
I. Muhammad Al-Shareef.
II. Title.
297.22

This book is an edited transcription and adaptation of Wings of Faith: Patience and Gratitude, a lecture by Dr. Omar Suleiman and Shaykh Muḥammad al-Shareef. All contents in this publication are adapted closely to the original work. The original authors are not responsible nor represented by any views, opinions or claims made in this work.

CONTENTS

FOREWORD 1

INTRODUCTION 3

CHAPTER 1: PATIENCE IS… 8

1. Certainty 9
2. Eternal 11
3. Rewarded without limit 14
4. Triumph 16
5. Being with Allah (s.w.t.) 19
6. A three-in-one reward 22
7. A human trait 26

CHAPTER 2: THE CATEGORIES OF PATIENCE 31

1. Physical patience 32
2. Psychological patience 45

CHAPTER 3: MANNERS OF PATIENCE **57**

1. *Rida* in *Qaḍa'Illah* 58
2. *Riḍa* with *Qaḍa'Illah* 62
3. Being Truthful in Patience 69
4. Disciplined in Patience 73

CHAPTER 4: GRATITUDE **76**

1. Fear and Hope 77
2. Patience and Gratitude 85
3. Always Be Positive 90
4. Allah (s.w.t.) Answers All of Our *Du'a'* 94
5. Patience and Its Silver Linings 96

FOREWORD

Ibn Qayyim al-Jawziyyah, the great scholar, once said: "*Iman* is of two halves; half is patience (*ṣabr*) and half is being thankful (*shukr*)." Simply put, you cannot truly complete your faith without both patience and gratitude. These are not strange concepts, yet they have been estranged from the modern world. The more technology has advanced, the deeper we have sunk into transient social and cultural trends, forgetting in the process the higher purpose we are meant to fulfil in this *dunya*. Whether due to apathy or ignorance, too many Muslims today have abandoned the ethical foundations of their *deen*.

This book represents one small effort to stem the ethical bleeding of the *ummah*. *Wings of Faith: Patience and Gratitude* seeks to remind the reader of the profound importance of these two actions—actions, yes, for patience and gratitude are not merely concepts to be understood, but ideals to be enacted. This book addresses the intricacies of patience and gratitude, as understood by the Islamic tradition, and highlights their symbiotic relationship: neither can survive without the other.

This book is adapted from a lecture of the same title delivered by Dr. Omar Suleiman and Shaykh Muhammad AlShareef. As such, just like both scholars, it conveys its message in both an academic and lay register. Readers will encounter rigorous argumentation structured around Qur'anic verses and *ahadith*, but they will also encounter light-hearted anecdotes. Even though the book is an edited transcript, the publisher has chosen to leave unedited many parts of the lecture in order to preserve the original voices of the speakers and thereby create a more authentic reading experience.

Tertib Publishing | tertib.press

INTRODUCTION

The story of Ayyub (a.s.) is one of the best stories regarding finding patience and courage, and no matter what generation you are from, the story remains relevant. It reminds me of my mother, because our heroes are often in our own homes—we just don't realise it. After all, we probably aren't paying attention. They do incredible things yet are often uncelebrated. But Allah (s.w.t.) celebrates them. My mother finished the Qur'an 14 times during her last Ramadan before she passed away. She was afflicted with cancer and multiple strokes, and each of her strokes took away some of her faculties. One of the strokes damaged her hearing, making her partially deaf. A second stroke took her speech, and a third her ability to walk easily. Her fourth stroke was the last one before she passed away.

If you met my mother, you know that she gave off an incredible sense of *sakinah,* of tranquillity. She was always smiling and had a lovely personality that was just out of this world. When she sat in a gathering, she rarely contributed because of her hearing difficulties, but she was able to smile, give *salam* and greet people. She would always say something like, "*Alḥamdulillāh*, Allah (s.w.t.) took my hearing because most of the things that people discuss during a social gathering are backbiting and gossip. *Alḥamdulillāh*, Allah (s.w.t.) protects me from that."

For me, that is how the story of Ayyub (a.s.) manifests in the *ṣabr* of the people we know and loved. More often than not, you do not have to search high and low in the history books to find an example of *ṣabr.* You can find it in the people in your own life. Just look around, and you can see extraordinary examples of patience and gratitude vividly illustrated by the people you know and love. We ask Allah (s.w.t.) to grant us the same capacity for patience. *Allāhumma amin.*

This collection of pages is an extension of and reflection on the Book of Patience by Imam Ibn

Qudamah, the author of *Mukhtasar Minhaj al-Qasidin*, which is itself the summary of Imam al-Ghazali's *Ihya' 'Ulumuddin* . It falls under the fourth section of the book, *al-Munjiyat*, which refers to the means of salvation. The final chapter, by Shaykh Muhammad AlShareef, is about gratitude. *Ṣabr* and *shukr* are our two means of salvation, the means by which we attain the pleasure of Allah (s.w.t.).

PATIENCE

[صبر]

Omar Suleiman

CHAPTER I

PATIENCE IS...

1. Certainty

Have you ever wondered how many times *ṣabr* (patience) is spoken about in the Qur'an? It is alluded to in the Qur'an in over 90 places. It appears, for instance, in verse 24 of Surah as-Sajdah:

وَجَعَلْنَا مِنْهُمْ أَئِمَّةً يَهْدُونَ بِأَمْرِنَا لَمَّا صَبَرُواۖ
وَكَانُوا بِـَٔايَـٰتِنَا يُوقِنُونَ

> And We made from among them leaders guiding by Our command when they were patient and [when] they were certain of Our signs.

The two most important qualities for a person who wants to lead are *ṣabr* and *yaqin*. *Ṣabr* is invoked in this *ayah* in the sense of resilience and steadfastness—being able to outlast your opponent or your hardship. This means being able to bear the course, no matter how difficult and bumpy the road gets.

The second one is *yaqin*, or certainty. If you have certainty in your mission and purpose, then that is the fuel that will keep you going long after other people have fallen. *SubḥānAllāh*, oftentimes they say that enthusiasm is a product of sincerity. However, sincerity is not always righteous. Someone might be sincere about something very evil. Since they are sincerely committed to that evil cause, they maintain a sense of enthusiasm. They can always go longer than everybody else. They can always go that extra mile. So here Allah (s.w.t.) says, leaders, if you want to lead, you need to have patience and resilience, and you need to have certainty—you better believe in what you have and what you are doing. If you have cracks in your belief, that is going to show when things become difficult. If a person seeks to lead in righteousness, they need to have the qualities of *ṣabr* and *yaqin*.

Patience and certainty.

2. Eternal

Allah (s.w.t.) says in Surah an-Naḥl, verse 96:

مَا عِندَكُمْ يَنفَدُ ۖ وَمَا عِندَ ٱللَّهِ بَاقٍ ۗ وَلَنَجْزِيَنَّ
ٱلَّذِينَ صَبَرُوٓا۟ أَجْرَهُم بِأَحْسَنِ مَا كَانُوا۟ يَعْمَلُونَ

> Whatever you have will end, but what Allah has is lasting. And We will surely give those who were patient their reward according to the best of what they used to do.

According to Imam Ibn Abbas (r.a.), Allah (s.w.t.) is saying that every single deed that is done here in this world, whether it is a good deed or hardship, stems from to the quality of patience. This means that when a person does a good deed with patience—for example, they have *khushuʿ* in their *ṣalah*—they make sure that they do their good deed right.

When hardship strikes and you show patience, the thing that is taken away from you—this is very powerful—still will be taken away from you, regardless. If it is not taken from you when you are living, it will be taken from you when you die.

This comes to the notion of *qadr* or not knowing the decree of Allah (s.w.t.). If you had a choice, let's say at the age of 25, to either be struck with a horrible disease or to be struck with death, which one would you choose? Most people would choose to have the disease. This is because they will think, *"I'll get over it eventually, even though I will suffer because I don't want to die. So I would rather face the hardship, hoping that Allah (s.w.t.) allows me to overcome it and face death when the time comes."* When we are struck with diseases, our health is taken away from us. That is all we can think about—the thing that is taken away from us. We are not realising that Allah (s.w.t.) spared us a life.

This brings us back to what Ayyub (a.s.) taught us about perspective. It could be that some *ṣadaqah* or charity that we gave or some good deed that we did to be the reason that Allah (s.w.t.) chose to extend our life to 80 years of age. But the only thing that we can see is *"I'm struck with a disease at 25."*

ʿAbdullah ibn ʿAbbas (r.a.), said, *"If Allah (s.w.t.) takes some of your wealth, health or something of this dunya, it was going to leave at some point anyway."*

مَا عِندَكُمْ يَنفَدُ

At some point, you will die and you will have no use or ability to take care of any of those blessings.

وَمَا عِندَ ٱللَّهِ بَاقٍ

But the good deeds with Allah (s.w.t.) stored in eternity.

وَلَنَجْزِيَنَّ ٱلَّذِينَ صَبَرُوٓا۟ أَجْرَهُم بِأَحْسَنِ مَا كَانُوا۟ يَعْمَلُونَ

And We will reward those who were patient with the best of what they used to do.

It is such a beautiful concept. Your *ṣabr* will stay. Anything that you lost, you were going to lose anyway. But if you show patience, that patience will meet you on the Day of Judgement and be the means for you to enter the garden of Allah (s.w.t.)—the means for you to enter *Jannah*.

3. Rewarded without limit

In the tenth verse of Surah az-Zumar, Allah (s.w.t.) says:

إِنَّمَا يُوَفَّى ٱلصَّـٰبِرُونَ أَجْرَهُم بِغَيْرِ حِسَابٍ...

... Indeed, the patient will be given their reward without account [i.e., limit].

The Prophet (s.a.w.) mentioned that when Allah (s.w.t.) rewards a good deed, He rewards it *bi ḥasab*, or within limits. In Surah al-Baqarah verse 261, Allah (s.w.t.) says:

مَّثَلُ ٱلَّذِينَ يُنفِقُونَ أَمْوَٰلَهُمْ فِى سَبِيلِ ٱللَّهِ
كَمَثَلِ حَبَّةٍ أَنۢبَتَتْ سَبْعَ سَنَابِلَ فِى كُلِّ سُنۢبُلَةٍ
مِّاْئَةُ حَبَّةٍ ۗ وَٱللَّهُ يُضَـٰعِفُ لِمَن يَشَآءُ ۗ وَٱللَّهُ
وَٰسِعٌ عَلِيمٌ

The example of those who spend their wealth in the way of Allah is like a seed [of grain] which grows seven spikes; in each spike is a

> hundred grains. And Allah multiplies [His reward] for whom He wills. And Allah is all-Encompassing and Knowing.

So Allah (s.w.t.) will multiply the good deeds of His righteous servants by 700 times or more, but ultimately there is a limit. But when it comes to *ṣabr*, Allah (s.w.t.) rewards *bi ghairi ḥisab;* Allah (s.w.t.) rewards without limit.

The Prophet (s.a.w.) said that most people will enter *Jannah* not because of the good deeds that they did, but because of their patience with the hardships that struck them. Can you imagine that? The majority of *Jannah*'s residents are *du'afa'*, *fuqara'* and *masakin*—poor people. People who were struck with poverty, people who had difficult circumstances in their life, but they were patient and Allah (s.w.t.) rewarded them *Jannah* as a result. The reward for good deeds is inherently limited, but the reward for *ṣabr* is limitless.

4. Triumph

In Surah al-A'raf, verse 137, Allah (s.w.t.) says:

وَأَوْرَثْنَا ٱلْقَوْمَ ٱلَّذِينَ كَانُوا۟ يُسْتَضْعَفُونَ مَشَـٰرِقَ
ٱلْأَرْضِ وَمَغَـٰرِبَهَا ٱلَّتِى بَـٰرَكْنَا فِيهَا ۖ وَتَمَّتْ
كَلِمَتُ رَبِّكَ ٱلْحُسْنَىٰ عَلَىٰ بَنِىٓ إِسْرَٰٓءِيلَ بِمَا
صَبَرُوا۟ ۖ وَدَمَّرْنَا مَا كَانَ يَصْنَعُ فِرْعَوْنُ وَقَوْمُهُۥ
وَمَا كَانُوا۟ يَعْرِشُونَ

> And We caused the people who had been oppressed to inherit the eastern regions of the land and the western ones, which We had blessed. And the good word [i.e., decree] of your Lord was fulfilled for the Children of Israel because of what they had patiently endured. And We destroyed [all] that Pharaoh and his people were producing and what they had been building.

As an individual, what can give you triumph on the Day of Judgement over someone that did much more good than you?

Patience.

Imam ibn Qudamah (r.a.h.) cited the above *ayah* to illustrate an important reality: You might have a small group of people who are weaker with fewer resources than their enemies, but so long as they have the quality of patience they can overcome much stronger foes. The greatest example of this truth is the *ṣaḥabah* of Prophet (s.a.w.), who in the battle of Badr defeated a far more powerful enemy.

The other example is fasting. Allah (s.w.t.) describes fasting in the Qur'an as *ṣabr*, as patience. Indeed, *ṣabr* is actually another name for *ṣiyam*, or fasting. For example, in verse 45 of Surah al-Baqarah, He (s.w.t.) says:

وَٱسْتَعِينُوا۟ بِٱلصَّبْرِ وَٱلصَّلَوٰةِ ۚ وَإِنَّهَا لَكَبِيرَةٌ إِلَّا عَلَى ٱلْخَٰشِعِينَ

And seek help through patience and prayer; and indeed, it is difficult except for the humbly submissive [to Allah]

Most of the *mufassirun* said that here the word '*ṣabr*' actually means fasting. Allah (s.w.t.) referring to fasting as *ṣabr* carries a special significance. Allah (s.w.t.) said, in a Hadith Qudsi, that all of the actions of the child of Adam are for himself, except for fasting.

الصَّوْمُ لِي وَأَنَا أَجْزِي بِهِ

> Fasting is for Me, and I will reward it accordingly.
>
> (Ṣaḥiḥ al-Bukhari 75380)

All of the good deeds that you do, are for you, and Allah (s.w.t.) will judge them with mercy. Fasting, however, is a special type of deed because there is no limit to how Allah (s.w.t.) rewards it. This emphasises إِنَّمَا يُوَفَّى ٱلصَّـٰبِرُونَ أَجْرَهُم بِغَيْرِ حِسَابٍ where the reward of those who are patience is limitless—and as fasting is a type of *ṣabr*, then the reward of fasting is also limitless.

5. Being with Allah (s.w.t.)

Allah (s.w.t.) reminds us in Surah al-Baqarah, verse 153, that:

إِنَّ ٱللَّهَ مَعَ ٱلصَّٰبِرِينَ...

... Indeed, Allah is with the patient.

Allah (s.w.t.) is with everyone in some sense because He sees and hears everyone. No one escapes the knowledge of Allah (s.w.t.) However, there is a difference between "Allah (s.w.t.) being with you" and "Allah (s.w.t.) being *with* you." Just as on the Day of Judgement, everyone will see Allah (s.w.t.), but not everyone will *see* Him. Seeing Allah when He is pleased with you in a special way is different from seeing Him as He judges you. What the above verse references, according to some scholars, is *'Al-Ma'iyatul Khasah'*, a special type of being with you.

In a Hadith Qudsi, it is mentioned that Allah (s.w.t.) says to a person on the Day of Judgement,

"I was hungry and you did not feed me." And the person responds, "*Ya Rabb*, how could I feed you? You are the Lord of the Worlds." Then, Allah (s.w.t.) says, "Didn't you, so and so, know that My servant, so and so, was hungry, and had you fed him, you would have found My reward with him." Then Allah (s.w.t.) says, "I was thirsty, and you gave me nothing to nourish me." And the person responds, "*Ya Rabb*, how could I give you something to drink? You are the Lord of the Worlds." And Allah (s.w.t.) says, "Didn't you, so and so, know that My servant, so and so, was thirsty, and had you given My servant water or drink, you would have found My reward with that person." And then Allah (s.w.t.) says, "I was sick, and you did not visit me." And the person responds, "*Ya Rabb*, how could I visit you? You are the Lord of the Worlds." And Allah (s.w.t.) says, "Didn't you know, so and so, that My servant, so and so, was sick, and had you visited him, you would have found **Me** with him".

(Ṣaḥiḥ Muslim 2569)

Not My reward, but Me.

So when Allah (s.w.t.) is with you, it is special. He will not empty your hands when you are going through hardships, except that He replaces it with Himself, which is a thousand times better than whatever it is that you lost. In the process of grieving the loss of something else, you found Allah (s.w.t.). This is something that Allah (s.w.t.) has specifically awarded to those who are patient.

6. A three-in-one reward

Allah (s.w.t.) also says in Surah al-Baqarah, verse 157:

أُوْلَـٰٓئِكَ عَلَيْهِمْ صَلَوَٰتٌ مِّن رَّبِّهِمْ وَرَحْمَةٌ ۖ
وَأُوْلَـٰٓئِكَ هُمُ ٱلْمُهْتَدُونَ

Those are the ones upon whom are blessings from their Lord and mercy. And it is those who are the [rightly] guided.

Allah (s.w.t.) combines for the patient three rewards:

i. Upon them is the prayer of the Lord [صَلَوَٰتٌ مِّن رَّبِّهِمْ]

Do you know what it means for Allah (s.w.t.) to pray upon us?

As Imam Ibn Qayyim (r.a.h.) described, it is when Allah (s.w.t.) mentions your name and praises you amongst the highest angels. How special is it when Allah (s.w.t.) mentions your name to praise you? How amazing is it that you find yourself in a conversation between Allah (s.w.t.) and Jibril (a.s.)?

Because if Allah (s.w.t.) loves someone, He calls Jibril (a.s.), and says, "I love this person, so you should love this person as well." So Jibril (a.s.) loves that person and calls out to the angels, and says, "Allah (s.w.t.) loves this person, so you all should love this person too."

Allah (s.w.t.) says those who are patient necessitate the love of Allah (s.w.t.). When a person is in the category of *as-Ṣabirun*, they naturally become amongst those who are beloved to Allah (s.w.t.) When Allah (s.w.t.) prays upon you, He places you in conversation between Himself and Jibril (a.s.) and the angels, all of whom love you.

ii. The Mercy of Allah (s.w.t.) [وَرَحْمَةٌ]

Raḥmah does not simply mean forgiveness. Allah (s.w.t.) calls *Jannah* His *raḥmah*. You are My mercy, I show mercy through you to whomever I will. So Allah (s.w.t.) says that you have His praise and heavens, and you have His mercy.

iii. The Guidance of Allah (s.w.t.) [وَأُولَٰٓئِكَ هُمُ ٱلْمُهْتَدُونَ]

You also have His guidance going forward.

The *ʿulama'* said that the prayer of your Lord (s.w.t.) refers to the present, to this moment. *Raḥmah*, on the other hand, refers to the past. This means that Allah (s.w.t.) forgives you for all your previous sins. Through hardships and trials, Allah (s.w.t.) purifies all of your sins, all while guiding you towards the future. Thus Allah (s.w.t.) covers your present, your past and your future. You have retrospective mercy and guidance that will change your life while at the same time, you receive the necessary adjustments to continue on that trajectory towards Allah (s.w.t.).

And as Ibn Qudamah (r.a.h.) says, there is no other category of people in the Qur'an that Allah (s.w.t.) combines for them in one verse His prayers upon them, His mercy as well as His guidance. That is why the Prophet (s.a.w.) talks about patience in the highest manner.

Abu Said al-Khudri (r.a.) reported that some of the people of the Ansar came to the Prophet (s.a.w.) and asked him for wealth. So the Prophet (s.a.w.) spent on them. And they came to him (s.a.w.) again, and again the Prophet (s.a.w.) have them whatever they asked. Finally, the Prophet (s.a.w.) ran out of things to give them. He (s.a.w.) said, "What Allah (s.w.t.) has given me of wealth, I will not hoard from you. But whoever has forbearance, Allah (s.w.t.) will help him. Whoever tries to be independent, Allah (s.w.t.) will enrich him. And whoever tries to be patient, Allah (s.w.t.) will give him patience."

And then the Prophet (s.a.w.) said, "No one is given a gift from Allah (s.w.t.), *khayran wa ausaʿu* than the gift of patience." *Khayran* refers to the fact that patience is better than any deed that you can prepare for Allah (s.w.t.) *Ausaʿu* means more vast or comprehensive—if you have patience as one of your qualities, it will benefit you in all aspects of your life. It will benefit you in acts of worship, your family relationship, your *duʿaʾ*, your worldly pursuits and even in the overcoming of your enemies.

Imam Hasan al-Basri (r.a.h.) said, Allah (s.w.t.) only gives patience to someone who is *karim* or noble to him—someone whom Allah (s.w.t.) truly loves.

7. A human trait

According to Imam Ibn Qudamah (r.a.h.), some of the early Muslims used to take a piece of paper and on it write Surah at-Ṭur, verse 48:

وَٱصْبِرْ لِحُكْمِ رَبِّكَ فَإِنَّكَ بِأَعْيُنِنَا ۖ ...

> And be patient, [O' Muhammad], for the decision of your Lord, for indeed, you are in Our eyes [i.e., sight]...

Some of the *salaf*, as a means of reminding themselves, used to write this verse on a sheet of paper and kept that paper in their pocket with them so that would always remember that they are watched, protected, and loved by Allah (s.w.t.)

Imam Ibn Qudamah (r.a.h.) argued that patience is exclusively a human trait. Imam al-Ghazali (r.a.h.) commented further on this, and it really is a powerful insight—patience belongs only to human beings. It does not belong to the angels or animals. Animals are not bound by patience. What makes them animalistic is that they eat their prey or whatever it is that they want without any type of limit whatsoever. And Allah (s.w.t.) has created them that way. When Allah (s.w.t.) describes people who do not have patience, He (s.w.t.) describes them as becoming like animals. So Allah (s.w.t.) says, you could be like a cattle, more astray than a cow. Allah (s.w.t.) also says, the example of a person who follows their lusts is like a dog with its tongue sticking out. If you put a bone in front of it, it will be panting and salivating. But, if you do not put a bone in front of it, it will still be panting and salivating. So when a person has no patience with his *shahawat,* or desires, then they become like that, tongue sticking out and blindly following desire whatever it may be. So Imam Ibn Qudamah (r.a.h.) says, patience is exclusively your *ʿibadah*, as a human being. It is your form of worship.

Remember that when the *shayṭan* challenged Adam (a.s.), or challenged Allah (s.w.t.) in regards to Adam (a.s.) and the children of Adam (a.s.), he said, as recorded in Surah al-Aʿraf verse 17:

وَلَا تَجِدُ أَكْثَرَهُمْ شَٰكِرِينَ...

...You will not find the majority of them grateful.

On top of that, when Allah (s.w.t.) informed the angels of his creation of Adam (a.s.) and humanity, they replied, as recorded in Surah al-Baqarah verse 30:

أَتَجْعَلُ فِيهَا مَن يُفْسِدُ فِيهَا وَيَسْفِكُ ٱلدِّمَآءَ......

"Will You place upon it one who causes corruption therein and sheds blood…"

In other words, the angels asked, will Allah (s.w.t.) create a people that will be overcome by their impulses and desires, until those desires are coupled with power becoming corruption? When corruption overruns the earth, it results in widespread slaughter. People begin killing each other for the sake of their limitless appetites for this *dunya.* Wars erupt everywhere.

The angels feared that human beings would lack *ṣabr,* while *shayṭan* claimed that human beings would lack *shukr*. Therefore, if a person is able to practise *ṣabr,* they will ascend in rank. On the other hand, when human beings practise *shukr,* they shame the ungrateful *shayṭan* who only worshipped Allah (s.w.t.) out of self-interest.

Imam al-Ghazali (r.a.h). also says that an *ʿibadah,* that Allah (s.w.t.) reserved for human beings, that he has not given to the animals, is *sujud* (prostration). We have been perfectly designed for *sajdah.* Our composition as human beings is to go into *sujud.* No animals can make *sajdah* the way we make *sajdah.* We thus have a capacity for *ṣabr* and *shukr*, and for expressing them, beyond any animal.

As Imam ibn Qudamah (r.a.h). observes, when you are born, you have one desire and one desire alone, which is eating. All you want is food, and that doesn't stop during your childhood. But when you are a child, your *shahawat*, or desire, is limited. When you grow up a little your desire expands beyond food to include entertainment. Then, later in life, comes the desire for money, wealth and sex. If you tell an eight-year-old that he will get married one day, what do you think his response? "Ew!" And some sisters might still say the same when reading this right now.

However, we need to admit that as we grow older, our desires, and our access to those desires, grow as well. As we become more independent, we become more capable of indulging our carnal desire.

Allah (s.w.t.) has designed us so that our mind, maturity, spirituality and reasoning all grow alongside our desires, at roughly the same rate. They all develop simultaneously, so that every step of the way we are able to choose what is right over simply following our *shahawat.* As we get older and our access to desire grows, so too does the reward.

CHAPTER 2

THE CATEGORIES OF PATIENCE

1. Physical patience

Ibadah (worship) sometimes inflicts physical pain and fatigue. To bear this pain is to exercise physical patience. It means, for example, to have *ṣabr* in your fasting. It is not easy to have patience in your fast when sick or fatigued. When the Muhajirun moved to Madinah, they all fell ill. The migration had been emotionally taxing, and many of them suffered from an overwhelming sense of homesickness. Even Abu Bakr (r.a.) and Bilal (r.a.) contracted an infectious fever. But the Prophet (s.a.w.) promised that he would be their intercessor on the Day of Judgement if they powered through the hardships in Madinah.

As narrated by Abu Hurayrah (r.a.):

> The Messenger of Allah (s.a.w.) said: "No one is patient with the difficulties and hardships of al-Madinah, except that I am an intercessor or a witness for him on the Day of Judgement".
>
> (Jamiʿ at-Tirmidhi 3924)

i. Patience in obedience

This brings us to *ṭaʿah* (obedience) in performing *ʿibadah.* As Allah's servants, we need to worship with patience. Laziness may lead us to detest some rituals, such as *ṣalah.* As Allah (s.w.t.) says in verse 142 of Surah an-Nisa':

إِذَا قَامُوٓاْ إِلَى ٱلصَّلَوٰةِ قَامُواْ كُسَالَىٰ...

...When they stand, they drag their feet towards the *ṣalah.*

Kasal (laziness) makes you impatient in your *ṣalah.* For people who want to achieve *khushuʿ* in prayer, the answer is easy: You need to slow down. Take a moment to learn what you are saying. Recite the verses slowly, and give the *ṣalah* its proper time. Reserve a few minutes before the prayer to prepare yourself mentally, spiritually, and emotionally. Slow down your movements, read slower, and you will see the difference that it makes in your *ṣalah.* But people may find it difficult to slow themselves down, especially considering the breakneck pace of modern life.

Fortunately, there are things you can do to cultivate *ṣabr* in your *ṭaʿah* and acts of obedience. Firstly, *istas-ḥihan niyyah*—renew your intention. Remind yourself why you are doing what you are doing. Every time you are going to engage in an act that requires obedience to Allah (s.w.t.), you need to first remind yourself *why* you do it in order to rectify your intentions.

During *ʿibadah*, a person must not slip into *ghafla*, or heedlessness. To prevent this, perform *dhikr* throughout your *ʿibadah*. Always know what you are saying. Be present.

Then, *an-ifsaʾihi*—do not publicise your worship. You should not rush to make people aware of your good deeds. This is typically in *ikhlaṣ* or sincerity. What does this have to do with patience, you may wonder? Imam ibn Qayyim (r.a.h). said something very beautiful:

"It's our nature as human beings to want to show off our good, our accomplishments.

However, the believer delays that moment and is patient for that moment until the hereafter."

What does this entail? Allah (s.w.t.), describing the Day of Judgement in verse 19 of Surah al-Haqqah, tell us:

فَأَمَّا مَنْ أُوتِىَ كِتَٰبَهُۥ بِيَمِينِهِۦ فَيَقُولُ هَآؤُمُ ٱقْرَءُوا۟ كِتَٰبِيَهْ

So as for he who is given his record in his right hand, he will say, "Here, read my record!"

Each one of us will be called to Allah (s.w.t.) on the Day of Judgement, and we will receive the Book of Records either in our right hand or our left hand. But the person who receives their book with their right hand, a sign of success, will flaunt their book, boasting, "Come read my book!"

Ibn Qayyim (r.a.h). said that this is natural for the believer. Just like what Allah (s.w.t.) said in Surah al-Muṭaffifin, verse 26:

وَفِى ذَٰلِكَ فَلْيَتَنَافَسِ ٱلْمُتَنَٰفِسُونَ...

... So for this let the competitors compete.

Competition is natural, but Allah (s.w.t.)

redirects the competition. Likewise, be patient with the showing off your good deeds. If you wait, you'll get your chance on the Day of Judgement. Whenever you get the urge to brag in this world, remember that moment on the Day of Judgement.

ii. Patience in persistently shunning disobedience

Back-biting and lying are sins, yet they are so easy to commit that they become difficult to avoid. If we were to see a brother wearing silky clothes, we would probably condemn him right away. But if we were to see that same brother indulging in backbiting, we would probably hesitate to issue a comparable condemnation. Both are examples of disobedience, yet people tend to be more comfortable criticizing the former than the latter. Why this inconsistency?

We live in an era where sins have become normalised, especially ones that are obvious and easily conducted. This opens a door for people who will take the liberty to indulge in those sins so long as no one else condemns them for it. *Ghiba'* (back-biting) in particular has become utterly normalised in our gatherings. Sometimes you see someone who is "religious" bad-mouth somebody else, so you engage with it and it becomes normal. "It can't be that bad if these 'religious' people are talking about a person like this," you think. People immediately lose themselves in these sins. If you think about how many WhatsApp conversations go sour, and how many houses are unvisited because of back-biting, then you will realise how badly this affects our lives. It has been so normalised because our tongues are loosening and we do not know how to restrain them due to a lack of *ṣabr* and discipline.

iii. Patience in tragedy

Last but not least is physical patience in the face of *al-masaib*, or tragedy—the involuntary losses that are completely out of our hands. Some examples include the death of a loved one, the loss of wealth, and being inflicted with disabilities. This patience grants you the highest station with Allah (s.w.t.) Its *sanad*, or chain, is *yaqin*, meaning this chain with Allah (s.w.t.) is based on your complete trust in Allah's wisdom, even if you yourself can't see it or understand it. This requires a complete submission of your affairs to Allah (s.w.t.)

The Prophet (s.a.w.) said:

Whomever Allah (s.w.t.) wants good for, He allows him to be tested.

(Ṣaḥiḥ al-Bukhari 5645)

Is everyone that is tested by Allah (s.w.t.) loved by Him? No. Some people are being punished instead. Is everyone who is not tested, not loved by Allah (s.w.t.)? No, not everyone that is loved by Allah (s.w.t.) will be tested—and not everyone that Allah (s.w.t.) tests, is loved by Allah (s.w.t.)

This situation is similar to another hadith:

Whomever Allah (s.w.t.) loves, He gives the understanding of the faith.

(Riyaḍ as-Saliḥin 1376)

Does this mean that every person whom Allah (s.w.t.) loves become a scholar?

No. Some of the people most beloved by Allah (s.w.t.) were illiterate. Other people had knowledge, but they used it for corrupt and dishonest ends. Indeed, the first people who will be dragged into the hellfire are the scholars. They abused or ignored the knowledge that Allah (s.w.t.) gave them. May Allah (s.w.t.) protects us from falling into this category. This hadith and the one before it are conditional, meaning they are restricted in their meanings.

One of the ways that Allah (s.w.t.) shows His love to a person is by testing them as a means of elevating them and expiating their sins. To practice *ṣabr* in the wake of tragedy is to affirm to Allah (s.w.t.) that you accept the loss in this world in the hopes of a reward in the hereafter. Simply put, *ṣabr* is when you take the loss in this world in preference for the gain in the hereafter.

But what if someone hurts you? That is when you replace your hatred for that person with love of Allah (s.w.t.). This is the concept of *ṣabr ʿala adha an-nas*—to be patient with people when they hurt you. By exercising patience with this emotionally difficult hardship, you prefer His pleasure and *riḍa* to your anger towards that person. It is another layer of reward.

As Allah (s.w.t.) said in Surah Ali-'Imran, verse 186:

وَإِن تَصْبِرُوا۟ وَتَتَّقُوا۟ فَإِنَّ ذَٰلِكَ مِنْ عَزْمِ ٱلْأُمُورِ...

...But if you are patient and fear Allah—indeed, that is of the matters [worthy] of resolve.

And in Surah as-Ḥijr, verse 97:

وَلَقَدْ نَعْلَمُ أَنَّكَ يَضِيقُ صَدْرُكَ بِمَا يَقُولُونَ

And We already know that your breast is constrained by what they say.

And in Surah an-Naḥl, verse 126:

وَإِنْ عَاقَبْتُمْ فَعَاقِبُوا۟ بِمِثْلِ مَا عُوقِبْتُم بِهِۦ ۖ وَلَئِن صَبَرْتُمْ لَهُوَ خَيْرٌ لِّلصَّٰبِرِينَ

And if you punish [an enemy, O' believers], punish with an equivalent of that with which you were harmed. But if you are patient—it is better for those who are patient.

This verse suggests that people have the right to revenge, but that it must be on par with what they have suffered. However, it is best to not retaliate and to be patient instead. The reason why *ṣabr* is used twice in this is that showing patience is the greatest reward for those who are patient.

In another hadith on a person who is struck by tragedy, the Prophet (s.a.w.) said:

"No fatigue, nor disease, nor sorrow, nor sadness, nor hurt, nor distress befalls a Muslim, even if it were the prick he receives from a thorn, but that Allah expiates some of his sins for that."

(Ṣaḥiḥ al-Bukhari 5641, 5642)

In this hadith, both physical and emotional pain is mentioned. This is powerful because oftentimes in our discussions we abandon emotional pain in favour of physical pain, even though the former can often hurt even more than the latter. It is relieving to know that Allah (s.w.t.) rewards patience in enduring emotional pain accordingly.

The Prophet (s.a.w.) said that believing men and women will suffer adversities in their bodies, properties, and children until they meet Allah (s.w.t.) completely sinless and purified. The Prophet (s.a.w.) used to seek from Allah (s.w.t.) protection from sudden death. Most of us, when we think about death, wish for the easiest and the quickest death—so why did the Prophet (s.a.w.) seek protection from sudden death? When a person suffers in their final moments, they purify themselves of past sins. That is a *raḥmah* from Allah (s.w.t.) for those who leave this life while undergoing some kind of hardship. He is giving them the chance to make *taḥlil* their last words.

In another hadith, the Prophet (s.a.w.) said:

"Trials will not cease afflicting the believing man and the believing woman in their self, children, and wealth, until they meet Allah without having any sin."

(Jamiʿ at-Tirmidhi 2399)

In a Hadith Qudsi, Allah (s.w.t.) says:

إذ وجهت إلى عبد من عبيدي مصيبة في بدنه أو ماله أو ولد

If I tasked one of my servants, with a tragedy in regards to their family, wealth or health

ثم استقبل ذلك بصبر جميل

And that servant of Mine responded with a beautiful patience

استحيت منه يوم القيامة أن انصب له ميزان

I am too shy on the Day of Judgement to unravel his scroll in front of him

How amazing is Allah (s.w.t.)? He, the Almighty, is shy of us. *SubḥānAllāh*, it is such an incredible concept. Allah (s.w.t.) is too shy to not answer you when you raise your hands and make *du'a'* to Him. As the Prophet (s.a.w.) told us, when those hands are raised, Allah (s.w.t.) will not permit them to come back down empty, without any answer. Likewise on the Day of Judgement, when Allah (s.w.t.) is shy to unravel their scroll in front of a person He has tested, perhaps that person will enter the *Jannah* without any form of *adhab*, *ḥisab*, or questioning.

May Allah place us amongst these people, *Allāhumma amin*.

2. Psychological patience

This type of patience covers many aspects of human endeavour, from chastity to courage, forbearance to asceticism.

i. Chastity

Firstly, *al-'Iffah* is chastity. The Prophet (s.a.w.) talked about controlling the desire for food and the desire for intimacy. This is a way of securing a reward from Allah (s.w.t.) This is powerful because of a common hadith from Prophet (s.a.w.) regarding how we eat:

Miqdam bin Madikarib said:

"I heard the Messenger of Allah (s.a.w.) say: 'A human being fills no worse vessel than his stomach. It is sufficient for a human being to eat a few mouthfuls to keep his spine straight. But if he must (fill it), then one-third of food, one third for drink and one third for air.'"

(Sunan ibn Majah 3349)

Most people will eat and drink as much as they can, leaving no space for air. So this is the patience that we talk about: to have control over our appetite for food.

The first innovation among the people after the demise of the Prophet (s.a.w.) was eating to their fill, with an unrestricted appetite unbefitting of a Muslim. Refraining from overeating requires a level of *ṣabr* as well. Overeating represents a lack of self-control.

It was narrated from Abu Hurayrah that the Messenger of Allah (s.a.w.) said:

"The believer eats with one intestine and the disbeliever eats with seven intestines."

(Sunan ibn Majah 3256)

What does this hadith make you think about?

It was reported that once a man came to the Prophet (s.a.w.) with the *ṣaḥabah*. He drank milk from seven different cows. The companions were shocked by this sight. The next day, the man embraced Islam and said his *shahadah*. Surprisingly, he only drank milk from one cow. Now that he was focused on Allah (s.w.t.), he suddenly he did not see a need to eat as much. He was now "distracted" by a greater purpose. So it can be said that part of *ṣabr* is self-control. You have to master your appetite.

The same holds true for sexual appetite. The Prophet (s.a.w.) talked about the benefits of holding ourselves accountable, guarding our private parts and our chastity. That is the practice of *ṣabr*. That is why the Prophet (s.a.w.) said, "O' young people, whoever amongst you can afford to get married, let them do so, but if they are unable to do so, then practise *ṣawm*, or patience". To guard your sexual appetite, you are going to need patience. You are going to need *ṣabr*.

ii. Courage

The second type of psychological *ṣabr* is courage. Imam Hasan al-Basri (r.a.h.) said, "Courage is being patient for an extra hour." This analogy is taken from the battle of Qadisiyyah, when one whole Muslim army was able to power forward and not take that break at night for that extra hour.

Some of you may know about Muhammad Ali (r.a.h.), a great boxer and a greater Muslim. His most famous fight was with George Foreman— "The Thrilla in Manila." At that time, George Foreman was a notorious boxer, while Muhammad Ali had been suspended from boxing for years because he refused to join the U.S. military. He was past the peak of his career, while George Foreman was just mauling people like a bear, beating them into exhaustion. No one was able to stand more than a few rounds with Foreman.

Muhammad Ali's fighting style was to be quick on his feet, but with Foreman he used a curious strategy. He let Foreman beat him until Foreman himself got tired. So if you watched that fight, it was just Foreman beating Ali over and over again, for seven rounds. But Muhammad Ali whispered to Foreman's ear, "Is that all that you've got?" And after seven rounds, Foreman said, "Yes, that is all I got." Then, Muhammad Ali knocked him out.

What this shows is that courage is being patient for an extra hour. A person can hold on and keep on going, far beyond what they think is possible.

It is such an incredible quality to possess, and it is often the difference-maker. Those extra reps that you did while exercising, during the time that you almost collapsed—that is *ṣabr*.

iii. Forbearance

The third one is *al-ḥilm*, or forbearance. This is taken from the context of being patient with someone else. It is much easier to be patient with a natural disaster than with someone who is offending you. The scholars said that this is the most difficult type of patience. The hardest type of patience is patience with people because people will drive you crazy.

The Prophet (s.a.w.) said:

> Knowledge is only by learning, and forbearance is only by forbearance, and whoever seeks good will be given it, and whoever wills Evil is prevented.
>
> (Al-Silsilah al-Ṣaḥiḥah, No. 342)

The scholars decided that the Prophet (s.a.w.) said this because he attained the most difficult traits. You can cultivate many good qualities, but how many people do you know overcame their bad temper? Even though they become practising Muslims, a bad temper is really difficult to cure. But the Prophet (s.a.w.) said that this is possible, with work and patience—*ḥilm.* Learn to be a little bit more patient at the restaurant with the waiter when they bring you the wrong order, when you are standing in the line and somebody cuts the queue, or when someone is being a bit rude to you. This will help you grow your forbearance.

iv. Asceticism

Az-Zuhud, or asceticism, is patience with wealth. A lot of people earn money too quickly, and they spent it too quickly as well. A great example of this is professional athletes. They suddenly get rich, and they end up spending all of their money and end up being poor. Celebrities, singers—it happens to most of them. So patience in this sense is a practice of *ṣabr* to save money, to be modest in your spending even though you have the capacity to buy whatever you want.

Sayyidina ʿUmar ibn Khaṭṭab (r.a.) once saw Jabl ibn ʿAbdullah (r.a.) with a bag of meat. So he asked about the meat and the conversation went like this:

"What is that, Jabl?"

"Meat."

"Did you buy it?"

"Yes, I bought it."

"Why did you buy it?"

"Because I desire it, I want to eat meat."

"Is it every time you desire something you buy it?"

There is nothing wrong with buying meat or buying nice clothes. But Sayyidina ʿUmar (r.a.) was making the point that just because you can afford it does not mean you should spend it. As such, learning to govern your spending is one branch of the practice of *ṣabr*. You may love video games, for example, but you know that a video game, when it first comes out, is expensive. You really love video games, but you can wait a couple of months until the price becomes more affordable. Say you recently got your iPhone 12, but then the iPhone 13 comes out. Enjoy that 12 for a little bit, don't rush to the 13. It is pretty much the same thing, with the same functions. That is a practice of *ṣabr*. Governing your spending is a psychological form of patience.

v. Allah's Unfolding Plans

In a hadith, the Prophet (s.a.w.) said,

"May Allah (s.w.t.) have mercy on my brother, Musa (a.s.). He was tested with something more difficult than this, and he was patient."

(Sahih al-Bukhari 3405)

In another hadith, the Prophet (s.a.w.) said:

"May the mercy of Allah be upon us and upon Musa. If he had patience, he would have seen marvels from his companion. But (Musa) said: 'If ever I ask you about anything after this, keep me not in your company: then would you have received a (full) excuse from my side."

(Sunan Abi Dawud 3984)

In this hadith, the Prophet (s.a.w.) is talking about Musa (a.s.) accompanying Khiḍir (a.s.). So Musa saw Khiḍir destroying a ship, killing a young boy and repairing a wall, as we see in Surah al-Kahf. All those acts were deemed deplorable and inappropriate, but they had their silver linings. And the Prophet (s.a.w.) said, if Musa (a.s.) was patient, he would have seen so much more. So even Musa (a.s.), who was exemplary in his patience with how he dealt with his people, fell short with Khiḍir (a.s.). He could not get over what he saw unfolding with Khiḍir (a.s.).

Many of us struggle similarly with Allah's unfolding plans. The Prophet (s.a.w.) mentioned a person who made *duʿaʾ* and just as the *duʿaʾ* was about to be answered, they said, "Allah s.w.t has forgotten me." Allah (s.w.t.) was going to deliver the answer to their *duʿaʾ* right then and there, but the person spoilt it because they were not patient with Allah's plans.

Yusuf (a.s.) suffered 21 years before he ascended his throne; Ayyub (a.s.) suffered an untreatable skin-eating disease for 18 years before being cured; and the Prophet (s.a.w.) only returned to Makkah, victorious, 21 years after his *daʿwah* began. Who can tell you what will happen when?

Before the Treaty of Hudaybiyyah, the Prophet (s.a.w.) had a dream of the Muslims doing *ʿumrah.* He thought it was a vision for that year, but it turned out to be one for the year after. Why didn't Allah (s.w.t.) give him that year? Only Allah (s.w.t.) knows. This is His wisdom, and we need to learn to be patient with it. Again, such patience is difficult—even Musa (a.s.) struggled to practice it.

vi. Completing a Task

Persevering in the completion of any given task is another type of patience. This is about resilience, about seeing things through. The Prophet (s.a.w.) mentioned this, particularly in the case of raising children. Kids are the greatest test of your patience. They will test you over and over again, because you do everything for them, and yet they grow up and become ungrateful. So *ṣabr* is seeing things through. The Prophet (s.a.w.) said:

"Uqba ibn ʾAmir reported that he heard the Messenger of Allah, may Allah bless him and grant him peace, say, 'If someone has three daughters and is patient with them and clothes them from his wealth, they will be a shield against the Fire for him.'"

(Al-Adab Al-Mufrad 76)

vii. Being calculating

الحلم والأناة

Being strategic and careful

Ḥilm is generally known as forbearance, or tolerating other people, as previously discussed. However, it can also be interpreted as being patient, in terms of a strategic and calculated person in doing things.

Once, while the Prophet (s.a.w.) was receiving representatives of different tribes, a man named Ashajj ibn Qays arrived late. He was the man who would stay behind to ensure that no one forgot their belongings, that all the camels were tied, and that all the jugs were filled—he was a perfectionist, making sure everything was done properly. Due to that, he came to the Prophet (s.a.w.) later than the others. The Prophet (s.a.w.) told him, "You possess two qualities that Allah loves. These are clemency and tolerance.'"

When we do things, we must do them perfectly, we do them right. We should not do things half-heartedly. Completing tasks as they should be completed, being strategic, being well-thought-out—all of these contain the quality of *ṣabr.* These things really transcend spirituality, don't they? They affect your family, your career, your diet, and your communal life. *Ṣabr* is so vast because it is meant to cover all of those things, not just one element. *Ṣabr* is something that you have to practise throughout all elements of your life if you want to realise it in your religion. If you are sloppy at work, it is very likely that you are sloppy with your worship too—due to lack of *ṣabr*.

CHAPTER 3
MANNERS OF PATIENCE

1. *Rida* in *Qaḍa'Illah*

إِنَّا لِلَّهِ وَإِنَّا إِلَيْهِ رَاجِعُونَ

Verily we belong to Allah and verily to Him do we return

This is called the *istirja'.* When anything unfortunate befalls the believer, the believer should say to Allah that we belong and to Him we return. We should keep silent, but also shed tears without disgust. To do otherwise is futile and only delights malicious people. Adversity should be endured with good patience without it being wrongly reflected in a man's behaviour. Thabit al-Banani said 'Abdullah ibn Mutarraf and his father dressed in good clothes and applied perfumes. Their people were outraged. "'Abdullah dies, and you do such and such?" He replied and said, "Should I give in to distress? Allah (s.w.t.) promises me with three traits, all of which are very dear to me." Allah (s.w.t.) said Surah al-Baqarah verse 156-157:

ٱلَّذِينَ إِذَآ أَصَٰبَتْهُم مُّصِيبَةٌ قَالُوٓا۟ إِنَّا لِلَّهِ وَإِنَّآ إِلَيْهِ رَٰجِعُونَ

Who say, when a misfortune striketh them: Lo! we are Allah›s and lo! unto Him we are returning.

أُو۟لَٰٓئِكَ عَلَيْهِمْ صَلَوَٰتٌ مِّن رَّبِّهِمْ وَرَحْمَةٌ ۖ وَأُو۟لَٰٓئِكَ هُمُ ٱلْمُهْتَدُونَ

Those are the ones upon whom are blessings from their Lord and mercy. And it is those who are the [rightly] guided.

He then said, "Verily I would spare everything taken from me in this world to have a reward in the hereafter. Even if it were a cup of water."

A similar narration is reported by Sila Abu Asham. His son joined the battle for the cause of Allah (s.w.t.), and he fought until he fell as a *shahid*, after which his father followed him to be *shahid* as well. And when the people went to his mother, she remarked, "Welcome if you are coming to congratulate me. Otherwise, return." If the adversity is concealed, it is purely divine bliss.

This is a tough one because if you are struggling and you need help, then you should seek help. But what is being condemned here is to complain of your adversity. This is where Ibn Qayyim (r.a.h.) remarked, "One man was complaining to another man over and over again." He responded, "You are complaining about the One who has mercy upon you to one who has no mercy upon you." In a similar vein, Sayyidina 'Umar ibn al-Khaṭṭab said there is no good in complaining all the time, for you will make your friends depressed and your enemies happy.

When we read these stories, we should take the lessons—it is not good to complain all the time. Instead, we should seek reward from it from Allah (s.w.t.).

Imam Ahmad (r.a.h.) was once asked, "How are you?" He said, "I'm good." The man said, "Didn't you suffer from a fever yesterday?" Imam Ahmad (r.a.h.) said, "I said I'm fine, so do not bother me with what I detest." What does this mean? Imam Ahmad (r.a.h.) is trying to *not complain* about his adversity.

These examples are far out there, so maybe we feel disconnected from them. But we must take the lessons from them. So consider the following:

Imam 'Ali (r.a.) remarked, "Out of reverence of Allah (s.w.t.), you should never complain to anyone or mention your adversity."

Ahnaf ibn Qays said, "I lost my eyesight for forty years but never mentioned it."

Syaqiq said, "Disclosing one's adversity impairs the sweetness of *iman* and what is in a person's heart."

When 'Umar ibn 'Aziz buried his son, he said: "All praises are to Allah (s.w.t.) who put you in my scales instead of me and your scale. May Allah (s.w.t.) have mercy on you, O' my son. You have honoured your father. By Allah (s.w.t.), I have been delighted with you since birth and I am not more pleased with you than ever before."

So this is about concealing your calamity, seeking its reward only from Allah (s.w.t.)

2. *Riḍa* with *Qaḍa'Illah*

What is *riḍa*?

What does it mean to be pleased with calamity? This is the most important part of this chapter. Delight in calamity is *sharʿie* rather than biological. It is not something that comes naturally. Human nature entails detesting adversities. Our human nature is to hate hardships. To tolerate and even embrace hardship is something that we need to strive to do. It won't happen without effort.

The Prophet (s.a.w.) said:

> "Whoever loves to meet Allah, Allah loves to meet him, and whoever hates to meet Allah, Allah hates to meet him." It was said to him: "O' Messenger of Allah, does hating to meet Allah mean hating to meet death? For all of us hate death." He said: "No. Rather that is only at the moment of death. But if he is given the glad tidings of the mercy and forgiveness of Allah, he loves to meet Allah and Allah loves to meet him; and if he is given the tidings of the

> punishment of Allah, he hates to meet Allah and Allah hates to meet him."
>
> (Sunan ibn Majah 4264)

For example, a sick man may seek a bitter remedy. He will spend a lot of money to get this medicine, and then he will take it and recover from his illness. He will be pleased with the recovery, not displeased with the bitter taste of the medicine. Imagine a king tells a poor man, "If I can strike you with a tiny stick, I will give you a thousand *dinar* for each one of those strikes." The poor man will be happy with the money that he will get, not concerned about the strikes. This distinction is very important. Oftentimes we mistakenly conflate being pleased with Allah (s.w.t.) despite our circumstances and being pleased with Allah (s.w.t.) *and* the circumstances. There are two conditions here:

i. **Being pleased with Allah (s.w.t.) despite the circumstances**

ii. **Being pleased with Allah (s.w.t.) and the circumstances**

The Prophet (s.a.w.) is not asking us to do the second. He is not asking us to *like* the test. That contradicts human nature. That is not what *riḍa* with *qaḍa illah* means.

The Prophet (s.a.w.) did not like losing his six children. He did not like losing Khadijah (r.a.). He did not like losing Abu Talib (r.a.). He did not like the circumstances, but he was pleased with Allah (s.w.t.) despite the circumstances. That is *riḍa*. That is what it means to be content with Allah (s.w.t.).

Sometimes we take it too far. Someone might say to a struggling friend, "You should like what is happening to you, you should just say *alḥamdulillāh* for it."

No!

You are saying *alḥamdulillāh* despite what has happened. There is a major difference between the two, and sometimes we mentally torture our friends when we try to give them advice on *ṣabr*. We make it seems like we need to like this hardship when we don't. It is not in our nature. The believer ultimately seeks to be connected to Allah (s.w.t.), and anything that can disconnect them from Allah (s.w.t.), they hate it. Anything or any way that can connect them to Allah (s.w.t.), they are pleased with, and they use that opportunity to come closer to Allah (s.w.t.).

Imam ibn Taymiyyah (r.a.h.), compared Fuḍayl ibn ʻIyaḍ and the Prophet (s.a.w.). Fuḍayl ibn ʻIyaḍ (r.a.h.) lost his son in a very unique way. His son's nickname was, "the one who is killed by the Qur'an." Why? The son, when he heard the recitation of the Qur'an, would become emotional, especially when he heard about hellfire. He feared it. If Fuḍayl (r.a.h.) was leading the *ṣalah*, and his son was behind him, he would not read any *ayah* about hellfire. So one day, he prayed and before he started *ṣalah*, he did not see his son there. So he read some of those verses about hellfire and in the middle of the prayer, he heard a thump. After the *ṣalah*, he saw that his son had passed away. His son had come to the *ṣalah* late, heard the verses, and passed away.

Fuḍayl was obviously distressed, but on the day

of the *janazah*, he had this big smile on his face. He was holding his head high, looking like a person in joy. Someone said to Fuḍayl, "This is not natural. It is okay to grieve." Then Fuḍayl (r.a.h.) said, "I want to show my pleasure in the decree of Allah (s.w.t.). This is my way to show Allah (s.w.t.) that despite my pain, I still love you and I am pleased with your *qaḍa*."

Ibn Taymiyyah then compared this to the Prophet (s.a.w.) when he buried his son, Ibrahim. He cried when he held him. ʿAbdur Rahman bin ʿAwf (r.a.) even asked, "You, too, O' Prophet?" Since he thought it was unbefitting for the Messenger of Allah to expose his grief in such a manner. And the Prophet (s.a.w.) said, "This is the mercy in the heart. This is the natural love and compassion in the heart." So the eyes shed tears and the heart is broken, but the tongue only says things that are pleasing to Allah (s.w.t.).

Now the question is, who had *riḍa* with *qaḍa illah*? Fuḍayl or the Prophet (s.a.w.)?

If you didn't know the names of the people involved, you might say, Fuḍayl had *riḍa*. He did not openly grieve. But Ibn Taymiyyah said that Fuḍayl did not. Fuḍayl was incapable of combining both the mercy that his heart held for his son *and* his *riḍa* with *qaḍa illah*, so he chose to focus solely on the *riḍa* part. This is because he knew that if he focused on his mercy and love for his son, sadness would overcome him. So he chose to immerse himself in that *riḍa* part. On the other hand, the Prophet (s.a.w.) was able to perfectly combine the compassion and mercy he had for his son with complete submission to and pleasure in what Allah (s.w.t.) had decreed.

Allah (s.w.t.) never demands you stop being human. You can be both sad and happy. These emotions do not have to conflict. Sometimes, our expectations of *ṣabr* are unreasonable, and they are not Prophetic. The Prophet (s.a.w.) did not ask us to deny our humanity. He asked us to amplify it. The most beautiful way is to be pleased with Allah (s.w.t.) despite it all. That is why even though it was *'Am al-Ḥuzn* (the year of grief) for the Prophet (s.a.w.) because he lost Khadijah (r.a.) and Abu Ṭalib (r.a.), his main concern was to preserve his connection with Allah (s.w.t.)

"As long as it is not a manifestation of Your anger upon me, then I am pleased with You, O' Allah."

So we ask Allah (s.w.t.) to grant us pleasure and *riḍa* in hard times and good times. To grant us self-control over our desires in our hardships. To allow us to have it emotionally and physically. And to allow us to have it in small things so that we have prepared ourselves for the big things. The Prophet (s.a.w.) said, "Whoever is not patient with small things will not be patient with big things." So each of these small moments of patience that you practised—in your work, family life, finance, time, and daily life in general, such as waiting in line or interacting with waiters—all prepared you for the big things. We ask Allah (s.w.t.) to not burden us with more than we can handle and to always find us among those who are grateful to Him in all of our situations. *Allāhumma amīn.*

3. Being Truthful in Patience

Imam ibn Qudamah (r.a.h.) said:

There is a righteous man who said,

A believer is patient in hard times, but no one is patient in times of ease and goodness except one who is truthful to Allah (s.w.t.).

When a person is in pain, how many promises do they make to Allah (s.w.t.)?

"O' Allah, if you deliver me out of this, I'm going to do this, this and that."

Allah (s.w.t.) then removes the hardships, but the promises only last three days. The hardship is gone, after all, so they feel like it is okay. They think, "My two or three days of the promise are good enough."

So, what does *ṣidq* or truthfulness in this saying means? Allah (s.w.t.) says in verse 23 of Surah al-Aḥzab:

مِّنَ ٱلْمُؤْمِنِينَ رِجَالٌ صَدَقُوا۟ مَا عَـٰهَدُوا۟ ٱللَّهَ عَلَيْهِ ۖ فَمِنْهُم مَّن قَضَىٰ نَحْبَهُۥ وَمِنْهُم مَّن يَنتَظِرُ ۖ وَمَا بَدَّلُوا۟ تَبْدِيلًا

Among the believers are men true to what they promised Allah. Among them is he who has fulfilled his vow [to the death], and among them is he who awaits [his chance]. And they did not alter [the terms of their commitment] by any alteration—

From those who believed, are those who are truthful to the covenant they take with Allah (s.w.t.) Some of them can fulfil their oath right away, and some of them are delayed in fulfilling that oath—meaning that they say they want to do something, but the opportunity to do that good deed does not present itself. But they don't lose their resolve. They say they will do something, they make promises with Allah (s.w.t.) and they fulfil those promises.

As-Ṣiddiq, a truthful person, has only one group of people above them—the prophets.

Imam al-Ghazali (r.a.h.) said, "*Iman* or faith gets you through the hard times. *Ṣidq* or truthfulness gets you through the good times."

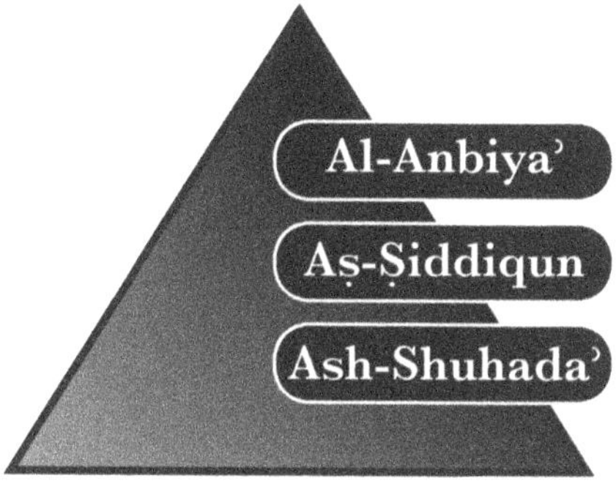

In your times of ease, you should remain just as dedicated to Allah (s.w.t.). You are not waiting for the hardships to come kick you from behind so that you can wake up and start doing the right thing again. Instead, you maintain your focus no matter your circumstances, good or bad. 'Abdur Rahman bin 'Awf (r.a.), such a prominent name for us, was the wealthiest of the companion of the Prophet (s.a.w.) His caravan, when it came to Madinah, shook the city with the number of animals that it carried.

He (r.a.) said,

ابْتُلِينَا بِالضَّرَّاءِ فَصَبَرْنَا

We were tested with hardships and we were patient.

ابْتُلِينَا بِالسَّرَّاءِ بَعْدَهُ فَلَمْ نَصْبِرْ

We were tested with ease and we fell short.

4. Disciplined in Patience

In verse 9 of Surah al-Munafiqun, Allah (s.w.t.) tells us:

يَـٰٓأَيُّهَا ٱلَّذِينَ ءَامَنُوا۟ لَا تُلْهِكُمْ أَمْوَٰلُكُمْ وَلَآ أَوْلَـٰدُكُمْ عَن ذِكْرِ ٱللَّهِ ۚ وَمَن يَفْعَلْ ذَٰلِكَ فَأُو۟لَـٰٓئِكَ هُمُ ٱلْخَـٰسِرُونَ

> O' you who have believed, let not your wealth and your children divert you from the remembrance of Allah. And whoever does that—then those are the losers.

This is *as-ṣabr 'ala ma yuwafiqil ḥawa'*. This is *ṣabr* that contradicts the self, that does not align with the desires of the self. This *ṣabr* requires discipline.

Imam Hasan al-Basri said: "The best definition of *ṣabr* is restraining the self." When hardship strikes, and you want to say something that is displeasing to Allah (s.w.t.), hold it, and say "*Alḥamdulillāh*" instead. Say "*innā lillāhi wa innā ilayhirāji'ūn*" instead. Hold yourself. That same mechanism plays out when you have easy access to some burning desire. It is easy for you to do it, yet you hold yourself. *Ṣabr*—you catch yourself.

The same principle applies when someone, after attaining power and wealth, becomes less tolerant of other people. Such a loss of compassion is almost natural. There is a hypothesis that the wealthier the person, the more easily agitated. They get upset more quickly, because they feel like they've got to a place where they shouldn't need to deal with incompetence or discomfort anymore. So *ṣabr* is to grab yourself and say, "No, no, no. Remember who you were."

Imam Hasan al-Basri describes this so beautifully as *habsun nafs*—knowing how to catch yourself.

GRATITUDE

[شكر]

Muḥammad al-Shareef

CHAPTER 4
GRATITUDE

1. Fear and Hope

We have to strive to become students of the school of *shukr*. Everyone has their Qur'anic mantra. Mine is from the seventh verse of Surah Ibrahim:

لَئِن شَكَرْتُمْ لَأَزِيدَنَّكُمْ

If you are grateful, I will certainly give you more.

Let me share a story with you. This was in the 1990s, the first time I performed *ḥajj*. My neighbours at Madinah University—one Libyan, the other Palestinian-Kuwaiti—were going to perform *ḥajj* on foot. They were going to do *ḥajj*, all of them, while walking the whole time, and they did not want to let me come with them. The reason was: I talk too much. I was around 19 years old then.

In literally the final hour before we were due to embark on *ḥajj,* I pleaded with them. "Please, we are in the same room. Can we go for *ḥajj* together?" They finally relented but on one condition: "Muhammad, do not talk. We are going to do everything walking, so we aren't going to ask your opinion about anything. We are just going to walk."

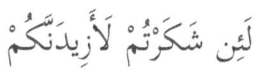

So we set out on *ḥajj*, and we walked a lot. Even from Makkah to Mina on the first day, we walked. I mean, there was no need for that because that walk takes about an hour and a half. We had not even started the *ḥajj*. One of us, the Libyan brother, was messed up. He was messed up because of fear and hope.

What is fear? Fear of the punishment of Allah (s.w.t.). What is hope? Hope in the mercy of Allah (s.w.t.) When you are performing your *ʿibadah*, which one do you emphasise? Think about this in a practical sense, based on how you go about your daily life. Are you more afraid of the punishment of Hell or are you more hopeful for the mercy of *Jannah*? Which one motivates you?

From my experience in the Muslim community in North America, we love to scare people. If you come to the *masjid*, you get horror and Hell. Then if you go to an interfaith event, you hear all these nice things about *Jannah*.

So while we were doing *ḥajj*, this Libyan brother, when he saw Muslims doing bad things, he started back-biting. He was muttering, "*Aʿūdhubillāh.*" When he saw a brother pulling out cigarettes, he said,

"*A'ūdhubillāh*, this is haram. How can he smoke in Mina?" This was day one of our *ḥajj*. This kept happening until eventually, this Libyan brother said something that hurt me. It hurt me so badly—like stabbed me in the heart.

Before I tell you what he said, I wanted to remind you of a hadith in which Allah (s.w.t.) declares his pride in the *ḥujjaj*.

> It was narrated by Abu Hurayrah (r.a.) that the Prophet (s.a.w.) said: "Allah boasts about the people of 'Arafah to the dwellers of heaven, saying, 'Just look at My slaves! They have come to Me with dishevelled hair and covered in dust.'"
>
> (Musnad Aḥmad, Ṣaḥiḥ ibn Ḥibban & al-Mustadrak al-Ḥakim)

And this brother, after observing the Muslims around us and their poor behaviour and bad habits, what did he say? He said to me: *"I don't know what Allah's proud of."*

At that moment I thought, I need to get you out of my life. But like I said earlier, I was not allowed to talk.

Now we were walking to ʿArafah, and I just had to ask, so I did, "What happens next?" But this brother would not tell me, because he said, "I told you not to talk." And *alḥamdulillāh*, on our way to ʿArafah, we lost him in the crowds. After we lost him, we did *ḥajj* by the book.

That was the hardest *ḥajj* I have ever done in my life. We did it exactly by the book, but between the crowds and the stampedes, there were several times that I thought I was going to die. On the last day of the *ḥajj*, it was me and the Palestinian-Kuwaiti brother. It was his first time doing *ḥajj* as well. So I said, "Hey, let's go to *jamrah*, wait till *Ẓuhr* time, throw our *jamrah* and then we will be done." At this point, I was in such bad shape—in pain and limping. I even saw some people from North America, and I wanted to say *salam* to them, but I looked at the state that I was in, and I thought, "I will probably scare them if they see me." So I just let it go.

We were sitting there at the *jamrah* and this was in the 90s, maybe 1994. There had been a stampede in the tunnel back when my father did his *ḥajj*. I thought to myself, "If a stampede happens, I will just move to a higher level. Then I will be safe." So we were sitting at the *jamrah* and it was close to *Ẓuhr* time, and then all of a sudden, we were lifted off the ground and slammed back down. It was like a tidal wave tore through the crowd. I saw people coming out, climbing up to higher ground, right behind me. And I thought, "I am in the stampede I have always prepared for." We lost the Libyan brother before, and now it was me and the Palestinian-Kuwaiti brother in this stampede.

What could you do? Could you just say, "Okay, timeout! I'm leaving"?

No. You had to go through it.

As soon as we stepped into the *jamrah*, I lost the Palestinian-Kuwaiti brother as well. I was on my own. People died that day, people were trampled on, sirens shrieking in the background, helicopters hovering about, and ambulances were everywhere. When I came to the end of the *jamrah*, I sat down because I was shell-shocked. Apparently, my back was resting against a sister's. I remember this moment because I did not know her. She did not know me either, and so we sat there, leaning our backs on each other. The whole situation with the stampede was so enormous, I barely paid the sister any mind. It felt as though the

Day of Judgement itself had arrived. Only after half an hour of leaning my back on this sister's back did I realise, "Hey, maybe I shouldn't be doing this."

I saw people coming out from the *jamrah*, looking for their friends, expecting their friends to have died. I saw three brothers who spotted a relative coming out, and one of them started shouting his name out of happiness. I was limping and I saw a Saudi man who had a villa near the *jamrah*, but I was too shy to request permission to enter, so I sat on the stairs to his house. This Saudi man—he had this carpet. Up until that moment in my *ḥajj*, I had not felt a carpet, and I said there is no *niʿmah* or blessing greater than this carpet. I sat there, trying to sleep by his door. This Saudi brother was looking out to the crowd of *ḥujjaj*, and he would find people who were limping and sick and he would run out into the crowd, grab them by the hand and bring them into his house, giving them water and rest. I sat there, on the stairs to his house, for three hours, but I was too shy to ask him for water. Then, I thought, I am going to die so I asked, "Can I have some water too?" because he was giving out water to other people. He then gave me some juice.

You don't know what a blessing these small things are until you don't have them. Eventually, I left the Saudi man and walked back to the Haram. I found the Palestinian-Kuwaiti brother, and I shared with him the good news. I reflected then on what the Libyan brother had said just a few days prior: "I don't know what Allah is proud of." I thought to myself, I had gotten a glimpse of why people leave the *deen*. I was 19 years old and thought to myself, "If Allah (s.w.t.) is never going to accept my *ḥajj*, then why am I doing *ḥajj*? If we all are going to go to hellfire in the end, why don't we just have fun instead of worshipping Allah (s.w.t.)?" I was young and I thought I was going to abort my *ḥajj*. After all, if Allah (s.w.t.) is the severest punisher, and there is no hope for you, then why are you here? Go have fun then, before you die.

But that wasn't it. I said to myself, if this Saudi man was so merciful with these *ḥujjaj*, what then of the Lord of these *ḥujjaj*? All these people only came to Makkah for *lā ilā haillallāh muḥammadu rasūllullāh*. There is nothing in Makkah. They only came to perform *ḥajj*, that is why you say *labbaykAllāh humma labbayk*. What else can you do in Makkah except pray? There is nothing to do there. It is just a valley. It is solely for worshipping Allah (s.w.t.).

So if this is how a human being will treat us, what then of Allah (s.w.t.)? Hence it is important to understand that both fear and hope ultimately go back to hope. To anybody who says they fear Allah (s.w.t.), I ask: does the fear lead you to hope? If not, then you are misguided. Fear has to lead back to hope. All the stories that you hear of righteous people worshipping Allah (s.w.t.) and invoking their fear of Him, they are crying at the door of the Ka'bah, calling upon the mercy of Allah (s.w.t.). The fear led to hope. It did not stop at fear. So fear and hope all return to hope, which is a beautiful thing.

This is a reminder for parents: whenever you scare your children, remember to never stop at the fear of Allah (s.w.t.) For example, your child is lying. "You can go to the hellfire for lying." Relax. "You can go to the hellfire for lying but Allah (s.w.t.) wants you to tell the truth and He loves for you to come back to Him." Always let that sentence continue to hope. It is not just "You will be punished" and "There is no hope for you."

2. Patience and Gratitude

So, regarding *ṣabr* and *shukr*. What if I tell you, after this long journey, that even *ṣabr* leads to *shukr*? What is true with fear and hope is true with *ṣabr* and *shukr*. All *ṣabr* returns to *shukr*. Patience return to gratitude. That is why the Prophet (s.a.w.) always said: "*Alḥamdulillāh*, thank you, O' Allah. All praises due to Allah." When something harmful or painful happened, what did the Prophet (s.a.w.) say? "*Alḥamdulillāhi 'alā kulli ḥāl.*" It all goes back to thankfulness. They say that *ṣabr* and *shukr* are two sides of the same coin. I say that *shukr* is on both sides of it.

Alḥamdulillāh, Alḥamdulillāhi 'alā kulli ḥāl.

I have a nephew. He is older now, not as cute as he used to be. When he was younger, he was so sweet—if you bought him a gift, he would say "Thank you." Not only that, he would say, "I love this gift, Uncle Muhammad, because you gave it to me." I thought, "Hold up, let me go get some more gifts for you." Then there is another child, when you give them a gift, they do not even recognise it is a gift. They do not realise they have just received a gift. They frown and they put it to aside.

Which of these two children do you want to continue giving gifts? You might be nice and give them both gifts, but at the end of the day, you really only want to give it to the appreciative child!

As Allah (s.w.t.) said in verse 7 of Surah Ibrahim:

لَئِن شَكَرْتُمْ لَأَزِيدَنَّكُمْ

If you are thankful, I will increase you.

If you chose to complain about things in life, what you are doing is cutting off the *khayr* or goodness from your life. Nine out of ten things you have that Allah (s.w.t.) gave you, you like them, but you will complain about that one thing that you do not like.

I am reminded that one time during *ḥajj*, everything was going smoothly. Nothing was wrong. But this brother, he complained. He was dissatisfied because of the *density* of the towels in his room. Another time, I was giving a lecture to the *ḥujjaj*, and a man stood up, angrily. He said, "It is good, what you are teaching right now, but when are we going to talk about the trash?" He was talking about the literal litter on the ground. Then I asked him, "Can you tell me what are the beautiful things you see in Makkah so far?" I put him on the spot, and he was dumbfounded and speechless. I mean, come on, you come to Makkah and you can't name <u>ONE</u> beautiful thing you see here? I asked, "How about the Ka'bah? Did you drink some *zamzam*? How about the people who are praying to Allah (s.w.t.) in front of the Ka'bah? Did you not see that as beautiful? Aren't you happy?" Then he said, "Oh. I did not notice."

When you always focus on what is wrong, all you can see is what's wrong. You will blind yourself to the good that surrounds you—to the *shukr*.

SubḥanAllāh.

I make it a habit that before I go to bed every night, I think, "Let me say *alḥamdulillāh* for every specific thing that happened today." I make sure my children do this as well. If we go to the playground, what happens when you have to take the children away from the playground? What do they say? "*Alḥamdulillāh* for the time that we spent at the playground. Thank you for bringing me, Mama and Baba. I hope to come next time, *inshā'Allāh.*" No! That is not what they say. Everybody knows every child leaves the playground crying. So this is what I do. My daughters cry when they leave the playground, and I make them sit down and I ask them, "Did the playground make you sad? Because if it did, I will never bring you back here again." *Alḥamdulillāh*, my daughters understood this. So they say, "No, Baba. The playground makes us happy." But not my sons. Not yet.

So for our own life, we have to be thankful for what Allah (s.w.t.) gave us and will continue to give us. Not only that, one of the issues that I care about a lot is *du'a'*. From the perspective of *du'a'*, if we want our *du'a'* to be accelerated, we should couple it with *shukr*. So we make *du'a'* and be thankful to Allah (s.w.t.) at the same time. A lot of times on social media, people are talking about *du'a'*, those stories of when their *du'a'* are accepted, everybody has their *du'a'* except one person. And it is interesting that one person who does not get his *du'a'* answered, is the ungrateful one. The Prophet (s.a.w.) said:

"All of you will have your du'a' answered, except the person who says, 'I made du'a', and my du'a' wasn't answered."

When I see people posting like that online, I think to myself, you are writing about your *du'a'* not being answered with that attitude. It is a self-fulfilling prophecy. *"My du'a' isn't answered."* It is not going to be answered. As the Prophet (s.a.w.) told us, if somebody approaches their *du'a'* and their connection to Allah (s.w.t.) saying I did not receive such and such, then they will not receive it.

3. Always Be Positive

Here is how we can apply *shukr* in our lives. This era, the era of the Internet and social media, houses so many complaining people. Instead of joining the chorus of complaints, try to be positive. Remember the *sunnah*. Parents, you've probably said this to your children: "The Prophet (s.a.w.) never belittled any food." You know the hadith. The Prophet (s.a.w.) never complained, even when he was displeased.

> Ibn 'Abbas said he was told by Khalid b. al-Walid that he went with God's messenger (s.a.w.) to visit Maimunah, who was both his and Ibn 'Abbas's maternal aunt, and found that she had a roasted lizard. She offered the lizard to God's messenger, and when he withdrew his hand from it Khalid asked him whether lizards were prohibited. He replied, "No, but there were none in the land of my people, and I find that I dislike them." Khalid said, "I then chewed and ate it while God's messenger was looking at me."
>
> (Mishkat al-Maṣabiḥ 4111)

If you looked at your spouse, husband or wife; maybe they are doing something that you disliked. But remember that Allah (s.w.t.) said in Surah al-Baqarah verse 216:

وَعَسَىٰٓ أَن تَكْرَهُوا۟ شَيْـًٔا وَهُوَ خَيْرٌ لَّكُمْ

Perhaps you dislike something which is good for you

Maybe you dislike it but it has a lot of *khayr*. So when your spouse is doing something that is disliked by you, and you are about to give an unpleasant response, remind yourself of the good and beautiful things in them.

I know it sounds so idealistic. But remember the very popular hadith:

Suhaib reported that Allah's Messenger (s.a.w.) said:

"Strange are the ways of a believer for there is good in every affair of his and this is not the case with anyone else except in the case of a believer for if he has an occasion to feel delighted, he thanks (God), thus there is a good for him in it, and if he gets into trouble and shows resignation (and endures it patiently), there is a good for him in it."

(Ṣaḥiḥ Muslim 2999)

People who have gone to *ḥajj* know this hadith. However, there is such a big difference between knowing this *hadith* and practising it in real life. You can go for *ḥajj* and see everybody losing it. You might ask them, "Oh, you don't know the hadith about patience?" And they will reply, "Don't tell me the hadith about patience right now!"

Everything that happens to a believer is better for them. If something harmful happens, they are patient so it is better for them. Something good happens, they are thankful so it is better for them. But after what I saw, with humans—hundreds and thousands of them, I would like to emphasise the final part of the hadith. It says:

ذَاكَ لِأَحَدٍ إِلَّا لِلْمُؤْمِنِ

This is only for the ***mu'min***.

So it does not apply to everyone—only to people who are working for their *iman*.

This is my practice, this is what I do. Whenever pain befalls me, I ask myself the question, "How is this better for me?" There was this time I dropped a bottle of Sprite. The lid popped off, the bottle hit the ground, and a second later my body was drenched in a Sprite tidal wave. You see, when a Sprite bottle explodes open, it releases a torrent of liquid that arcs up towards the ceiling and then rains back down on you and your clothes. When that happened, my first thought was, "HOW WILL THIS BENEFIT ME?" That's how I reacted. That is how I always react to harmful situations. It is automatic—how is this better for me?

I believe in this because the Prophet (s.a.w.) said so. Everything that happens to a believer is good for them. Maybe I cannot immediately tell how what happened is good for me. It is my responsibility to figure that out. For example, if a brother or a sister is not yet married, think, how is this better for me? When we are going through some struggle, think, how is this better for me? Your attitude will start to change. Then when you approach this situation with an attitude of *shukr*, your mindset, attitude and focus change, leading to the change in your situation.

4. Allah (s.w.t.) Answers All of Our *Du'a'*

In verse 60 of Surah Ghafir, Allah (s.w.t.) says:

وَقَالَ رَبُّكُمُ ٱدْعُونِىٓ أَسْتَجِبْ لَكُمْ

And call upon Me, I will answer you.

So when you make a *du'a'* to Allah (s.w.t.), all your *du'a'* are answered. I do not like it when I hear a person saying "I made a *du'a'* and my *du'a'* isn't answered," when something bad happens to them. I would like to say to them, "You know what? All your *du'a'* were answered."

Let me give an analogy. When a person asks me, "Hey, can you give me (something)?" Then I say, "I have something better for you. The thing that you are asking is not good for you. The thing I have for you is better." That has happened to you, right?

It is the same as what we request through *du'a'*. Sometimes, there are better things than what we are asking for. So when we do not get what we asked, it does not mean our *du'a'* is not answered. It means that

Allah (s.w.t.) answered with, "I have something better for you." I myself get a glimmer of excitement when Allah (s.w.t.) does not give me what I asked for. Why? Because it means Allah (s.w.t.). is going to give me something way than whatever I asked for.

Some other times, Allah (s.w.t.) answers your *du'ā'* with, "Not now, but later." This is because that very thing we asked might hurt us if we have it now, but it will bring good if we have it later. So all of our *du'ā'* are answered, and we need to have *shukr* for that.

Allah (s.w.t.) is more than anything that you can ask for, so you have to be thankful for that. Whatever happens in your life, you always say, "*Alḥamdulillāh.*" Not just in good times but in difficult moments as well —"*Alḥamdulillāhi 'alā kulli ḥāl.*"

5. Patience and Its Silver Linings

Whenever I make *ḥajj*, I am very serious with my group about patience. I do not like complaining. The one thing I have no patience for during *hajj* is people who are not patient. I tell them, "If you see me in *ḥajj*, and I'm cool and I'm just chilling, you don't need to be anxious," because some people get anxious for no reason. "But if you see me anxious and scared, you need to be scared."

Once, I was in this group of *ḥujjaj* from the U.S. and Canada, and *alḥamdulillāh* they had already taken lessons before *ḥajj*, but everything difficult in *ḥajj* that can happen, happened to the group. The bus broke down on the way to Makkah, so they had to call for another bus from Madinah, they arrived at their hotels but their rooms were not ready, somebody paid for something but it was not there—everything difficult that you can imagine. *Alḥamdulillāh*, the group was patient. They were encouraging one another, reminding each other to remain patient.

On the Day of *'Arafah*, in Mina, people were getting on the buses, getting ready to go to *'Arafah*. I told my group to stay calm. Everybody sat in the tent and just waited until we all got to the buses. Now, *'Arafah* begins after *Zuhr*, around 12:30. And *ḥajj* is *'Arafah*. If you are performing *ḥajj*, and you do nothing but *'Arafah*, you are considered to have performed your *ḥajj*. You have ways to make up the other parts. But if you did everything but *'Arafah*, there is no *ḥajj* for you. You are not considered to have performed *ḥajj*. *'Arafah* is that significant—going to *'Arafah*, after *Zuhr* on the ninth of *Dhul-ḥijjah*, is *ḥajj*.

So we were sitting as a group, in our tent in Mina, which is about 10 kilometres away. Time passed—9, 10, 11, 11:45, but still no buses. People began leaving on foot. Soon we were the only ones there. Around 11:50, some of the brothers asked, "Hey, can we just walk?" It would take about three hours to get to *'Arafah* on foot, by which time we would be dehydrated. Our group included pregnant sisters and people in wheelchairs, so we could not go walking. But those brothers did not want to wait any longer, so they decided to go ahead and walk it. They embarked on their three-hour walk in the smouldering heat, just 45 minutes before the start of *'Arafah*. The rest of them stepped out of the tent and looked around. It was empty. Everyone just stood there, their faces downcast.

So I said, "Listen. This is what we are dealing with right now. *'Arafah* is so close, but it is so far. We cannot go walking, because there are pregnant sisters and people in wheelchairs and it is 10 kilometres in the heat. Even if you arrived, you would be too exhausted. We did not do anything wrong. This whole *ḥajj* was exemplified by everybody in this group being patient. And now we are hit by the biggest test. There will be no *ḥajj* for us. I have this principle: the bigger the test, the bigger the opportunity for *Jannah*. But only if you are patient and thankful through that transition. This test is so big. We will go home with no *ḥajj*. Nobody says anything, and nobody curses or gets angry. Go back to the tent and make *du'a'* to Allah (s.w.t.) or make your *du'a'* here." The whole group was crying and nodding their heads, saying, "We will be patient." I was not crying, I was telling them the way it is. "We will be patient, and this is a matter of principle to me. Put your foot down. We are going back to the tent." I turned around after we all agreed that we were going to spend the day of *'Arafah* day right there, in Mina.

There would be no *ḥajj* for us. We all accepted that.

I returned to the tent, but suddenly the group leader was shouting, "Muhammad, come! The buses are waiting outside." So I told the group, "Let's go, the buses are here." Everybody was confused. That was when I started crying. That moment when you are patient and thankful—Allah (s.w.t.) is waiting for that moment. So many stories in the Qur'an tell us of such moments. When you are patient and thankful, Allah (s.w.t.) will open the door for you—He will part the seas for you, as he did for Musa (a.s.)

He (s.w.t.) is waiting for you.

We got on the bus, and do you know how quickly we reached *'Arafah*? Six minutes. We got there in six minutes because everybody else was at *'Arafah* already. The roads were empty. In the buses, we were crying and saying our *talbiyyah*, and when we reached the tents in *'Arafah*, people were just waking up, but we were at the highest state of *iman*. We were ready for the day of *'Arafah*. As for the brothers who were patient but left, they were there waiting for us when we got there. They said that as soon as they came out, somebody picked them up on the bus. So again, regarding *ṣabr* and *shukr*, it always goes back to *shukr*. And with hope and fear, it always comes back to hope and mercy of Allah (s.w.t).

www.ingramcontent.com/pod-product-compliance
Lightning Source LLC
LaVergne TN
LVHW061619070526
838199LV00078B/7344
* 9 7 8 9 6 7 2 8 4 4 1 9 8 *